T0077985

# Standards for Authentic Learning Experiences

"Strength Derived From Unity"
The Gift From Grace

DELFIN MERLAN, Ed.D
CARR WHEAT, Ed.D

authorHOUSE

*AuthorHouse™*
*1663 Liberty Drive*
*Bloomington, IN 47403*
*www.authorhouse.com*
*Phone: 833-262-8899*

*Published by AuthorHouse   04/22/2022*

*ISBN: 978-1-6655-5526-5 (sc)*
*ISBN: 978-1-6655-5525-8 (e)*

*Library of Congress Control Number: 2022905498*

*Print information available on the last page.*

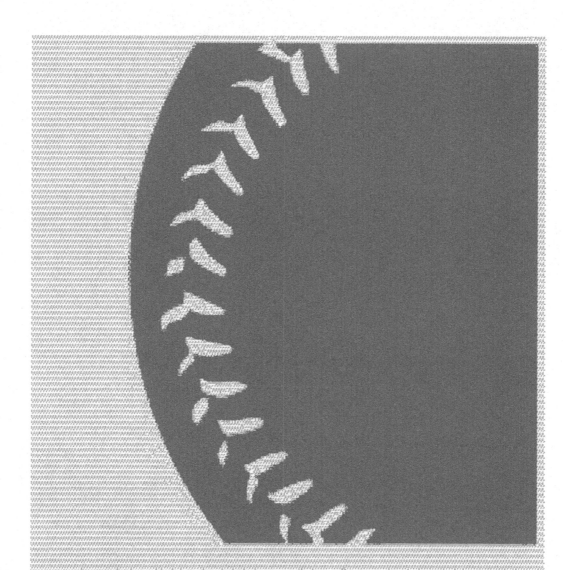

# AUTHENTIC
## LEARNING EXPERIENCES

# PSALM 23 KJV

*A Psalm of David.*

*1The LORD is my shepherd; I shall not want.*

*2He maketh me to lie down in green pastures:*

*He leadeth me beside the still waters.*

*3He restoreth my soul:*

*He leadeth me in the paths of righteousness for his name's sake.*

*4Yea, though I walk through the valley of the*

*shadow of death, I will fear no evil:*

*for thou art with me; Thy rod and thy staff they comfort me.*

*5Thou preparest a table before me in the presence of mine*

*enemies: Thou anointest my head with oil; my cup runneth over.*

*6Surely goodness and mercy shall follow me all the days of*

*my life: And I will dwell in the house of the LORD for ever.*

# Introduction & Purpose

Mission is to provide leaders the materials, tools, and resources to form a culture of success for teams and individuals to accomplish their mission, vision, and values. Authentic Learning Standards support Authentic Learning Practice to ensure leadership consistently Designs Knowledge, Actions, and Alliances.

Great leadership starts with developing a culture for all participants to feel empowered. When the leader develops a culture where participants feel welcomed, valued, and are inclusive of the process, then an Authentic Learning Experience (ALXP) thrives. Four years of research discovered a universal path authentic leaders follow that develops an authentic learning experience for team members.

This Standards Guide provides characteristics and behaviors Authentic Leaders use to build successful individuals and teams. Below are the purpose and goal of developing an Authentic Learning Experiences Culture/ Standards.

**Purpose:** Increase positive leadership behaviors by providing behaviors and characteristics of authentic leadership.

**Goal:** Develop successful sustainable and mindful cultures.

# Team Development Matrix

| | | | |
|---|---|---|---|
| | | | Effective<br><br>**5. Delegates Responsibilities** |
| | | Sharing<br><br>**3. Situational Learning**<br><br>**4. Partnerships** | |
| | Fractionated<br><br>**2. Safety** | | |
| Immature<br><br>**1. Purpose** | | | |

Interdependence

*Relationship*                                     Cohesion
*Behaviors*

                Conflict

                       Dependency

| Orientation | Organization | Open Data Flow | Problem Solving |
|---|---|---|---|

*Task Behaviors*

# Authentic Leadership Outcomes

1) The Leader demonstrates the authentic leadership attributes to develop high-performing teams.

2) Leaders create an environment/culture for members in the organization to feel valued, respected, and heard. Emotional Intelligence is displayed resolving conflicts in a positive and constructive manner for growth to occur.

3) Information and learning is shared openly. Ideas are generated and constructively analyzed as a potential solution.

4) Leaders develop positive interdependence within the team. Members enjoy being a part of the team and have fun.

5) Leaders are mindful and develop awareness throughout the organization.

6) Positive perceptions are developed throughout the organization.

# Key 1: Purpose

1) Leaders understand the significance of the alignment of purpose, and can differentiate various perspectives.

2) Leaders communicate their purpose consistently and effectively balancing the task and relationship behaviors. The team creates goals, roles, norms, values and expectations.

3) Leaders support their values with their actions to support their purpose.

4) Leaders display Emotional Intelligence (EQ).

5) Leaders effectively gain support for the purpose of the team. The purpose is seen through actions, words, and behaviors.

Non-verbals represent more than 80% of communications. Our actions speak louder than our words.

# Key 2: Safety

1) Leaders develop safe (physically, socially, psychological, and emotional) environments.

2) Leaders form fun and motivating environments to reduce stress.

3) Leaders set realistic and challenging goals.

4) Leaders understand sources of conflict and how to intervene with various strategies.

5) Leaders apply various coaching styles.

 Delfin Merlan, Ed.D; Carr Wheat, Ed.D

# Key 3: Situational Learning

1) Leaders foster partnerships throughout the organization.

2) Leaders gather input and provide feedback. Various sources are used to determine the needs of the team and individuals.

3) Leaders teach various roles and responsibilities within the team.

4) Leaders are organized and are effective administrators.

5) Information is shared openly.

# Key 4: Partnerships

1) Leaders implement appreciative-inquiry cycles of coaching based on the individual's needs.

2) Leaders utilize situational learning to teach lessons. He/She creates a fun learning environment.

3) Leaders understand the strengths of the team members.

4) Leaders have tools, resources, and strategies to move the group forward or backward through the Team Development Matrix.

5) Leaders develop trusting relationships in teams and provide beneficial feedback.

Delfin Merlan, Ed.D; Carr Wheat, Ed.D

# Key 5: Delegates Responsibilities

1) Leaders engage participants in the process of self-discovery and learning.

2) Leaders empower and motivate others to take action and problem solve.

3) Leaders provide roles and responsibilities for members in the organization.

4) Leaders develop positive perceptions throughout the organization. Inquiry based questions are used to reflect and move forward.

5) Leaders accomplish and exceed team goals.

# *Standards*

**1.0** *Purpose* Leaders understand the significance of the alignment of purpose, and can differentiate various perspectives. Leaders communicate their purpose consistently and effectively balancing the task and relationship behaviors. The team creates goals, roles, norms, values and expectations. Leaders support their values with their actions to support their purpose.

1.2    Leaders display Emotional Intelligence (EQ).

1.3    Leaders effectively gain support for the purpose of the team.

1.4    The purpose is seen through actions, words, and behaviors.

1.5    The purpose is communicated verbally, in letters, policies, contracts, and agreements.

1.6    The purpose is enthusiastically communicated when teaching.

1.7    The purpose is utilized through an individual-centered approach.

1.8    The purpose is applied through a holistic approach based on the learners needs.

1.9 Lessons on purpose are demonstrated interchangeably and interwoven throughout the day.

1.10 Age appropriate stories and experiences are shared to teach life lessons. Activities are designed to teach life lessons with an emphasis on character building.

1.11 Leaders understand the misalignment of goals can lead to issues due to differing perspectives. Leaders show empathy and redirect the focus through inquiry-based questions of participants when the purpose is misaligned.

1.12 Leaders model appropriate behaviors in all aspects when coaching, while maintaining ethical conduct during various settings (practices, meetings, competition, disagreements).

**2.0** *Safety* is exhibited through psychological, physical, social, and emotional practices. The leader is responsible for the well-being of the participants and recognizes conditions leading to unsafe practices.

2.1 Safety is a top priority when developing programs. The leader emphasizing and communicating age appropriate practices demonstrate routines to prevent overuse injuries and burnout.

2.2 Safety is communicated through the organization, verbally, written letters, policies, contracts, and agreements.

2.3 Positive feedback utilizes a minimum of 10 positives to 1 negative ratio to develop emotional strength.

2.4 Corrective feedback is used in a respectful and instructive manner so participants are encouraged and motivated to act.

2.5 The use of inquiry-based questions is practiced to correct errors or mistakes.

2.6 Preventative practices are taught prior to the start of each event, such as nutrition, physical conditioning, stretching, and pre-game routines to reduce stress.

2.7 Leaders use and monitor goals, schedules, logs, and lessons to ensure overuse injuries and burnout does not occur.

2.8 A socially responsible environment where participants are encouraged to take risks and learn from trial and error is formed due to modeling and feedback provided.

2.9 Leaders teach responsible decision-making by providing choices for participants.

2.10 Leaders demonstrate emotional intelligence understanding the various needs of each individual by listening to individual needs.

2.11 Leaders foster strong (psychological, physical, social, and emotional) team bonds for high-performance to occur by developing situational learning for teams to participate in.

2.12 Leaders create fun and motivating learning environments to reduce stress by focusing on having fun during competitions.

2.13 Leaders are perceived as caring, supportive, and motivational leaders concerned for the safety and well-being of the participants.

**3.0** *Situational Learning* are formed when the leader gains support for the organization by communicating, organizing and administering the practices of the organization effectively. The leaders Emotional Intelligence forms sustainable partnerships throughout the organization by carefully planned designs and implementation of objectives. Issues are overcome during interactions as the leader consistently demonstrates the values of the organization through the use of Emotional Intelligence.

3.1 Leaders apply the practices of Emotional Intelligence by listening and reacting appropriately.

3.2 Various roles and responsibilities are taught to participants.

3.3 Leaders use Co-Active Coaching or Confrontational Coaching based on the needs of the team or individuals.

3.4 Character building traits are taught, such as hard work, dedication, teamwork, practice, resiliency, and patience as the focus during drills.

3.5 Leaders model the desired behaviors and skills to demonstrate their beliefs to the members throughout the organization.

3.6 Age appropriate techniques are provided with individualized, small group, and whole group instruction.

3.7 Collaborative groups and competitive groups are used to facilitate learning.

3.8 Heterogeneous and homogeneous groups are woven throughout practice sessions to motivate and engage students.

3.9 Repetition is used in safe doses to ensure overuse injuries and burnout does not occur.

3.10 A positive learning culture is formed as the leader uses games, trial and error, and experiential learning providing new opportunities for participants to engage and try.

3.11 A balance of fun and work becomes the culture as children are seen communicating, laughing, sharing stories, questioning each other, and role-playing.

3.12 Knowledge is facilitated throughout the organization rather than seen as the experts of knowledge.

3.13 Guest speakers are brought in to share knowledge and motivate.

3.14 Family members, community members, and groups are seen contributing to the organization in some manner to reach the goals and purpose of the organization.

**4.0** *Partnerships* : Participants are building internal representation of the knowledge and interpretation of personal experience gained. Leaders engineer situations for individuals and teams to problem solve by providing an atmosphere of trial and error through practice. Members learn to deal with conflict, engage in problem solving, and seek positive solutions. By nurturing leadership potential, through social-constructivist practices, high-performing teams are formed due to participants critically engaging in the subject.

4.1 Participants are assigned new problems, situations, and experiences to problem solve and learn.

4.2 The leader engineers problems for participants to engage and participate in.

4.3 The use of Appreciative Inquiry is demonstrated and applied with participants.

4.4 Strength based approaches are used to foster growth and development.

4.5 Action research is used to check for understanding and the growth and development of skills.

4.6 Relationships are formed to foster motivation so feedback can be provided.

4.7 Parent(s) and guardians are an integral part in having the participant practice learning. The parent(s)/guardian stimulates the learning by understanding the expectations of the leader by reviewing the learning outside of the environment.

4.8 The leader evaluates and analyzes improvements for individuals and teams to be made.

4.9 The leader communicates the evaluation process to motivate participants.

4.10 Participants are encouraged to have fun learning, and motivated improve and share knowledge with their peers.

4.11 Mistakes are seen as opportunities for learning.

**5.0 Delegates Responsibility:** Empowerment can best be seen when followers are motivated to act. They challenge theories, reflect on personal assumptions, transfer insight and knowledge, engage in the process of problem solving, and they collaboratively work to solve problems. Tools and resources are provided to develop future leaders, and to enhance leadership skills. The leader engages in mentoring others. A learning culture promotes and delegates responsibilities to strengthen individuals, teams, and subsequently the organization.

5.1 Clear guidelines are provided for participants to follow

5.2 The use of mentors and captains can be seen to develop teams.

5.3 Responsibilities are delegated throughout the organization including youth, parents, and community members.

5.4 Responsibilities help reach the goals of the organization.

5.5 Responsibilities are communicated through emails, letters, web pages, and verbally.

5.6 Participants learn to develop, practice, monitor, and attain goals.

5.7 Leaders mentor and check progress of goals.

5.8 Leader challenge old assumptions by modeling and questioning outdated practices.

5.9 Opportunities are provided for participants to take on leadership roles.

5.10 Action learning cycles are formed to check for progress and improvement.

5.11 Teamwork and interdependence are seen as individuals work collaboratively to reach individual and team goals.

Figure 2 'Strength Derived From Unity' The symbol of a baseball comes from the strength of baseball woven together.

Authentic Learning Experiences studies the application of authentic learning principles, a proven real-time problem-based model to grow and develop empowering cultures of change.

In education to attain high-performance, play can be implemented through recreational and sporting activities (hobbies) to increase engagement, participation, and independence leading to higher performance. Ultimately, this will reduce the issues, arguments, and violence in youth sporting events. The standards provide a framework for leaders, participants, and members to demonstrate in their organization to foster authentic learning experiences.

AUTHENTIC
LEARNING EXPERIENCES

# Key 1

# Purpose Self-Assessment Rating

**1: Needs More Work**    **2: Communicated**
**3: Buy-In**            **4: Great Start**

| Stage 1 | 1 | 2 | 3 | 4 | Notes |
|---|---|---|---|---|---|
| Time was spent developing the relationship of the group. | | | | | |
| Time was spent getting to know the individual strengths of the team. | | | | | |
| The purpose was clearly identified and easily understood by all members on the team. | | | | | |
| The goals of the team were clearly communicated. | | | | | |
| The members of the team understand their role(s). | | | | | |
| The team norms were developed. Each member on the team understands how we will work and treat each other if an issue arises. | | | | | |
| This meeting was a good beginning. | | | | | |
| The team members rated this meeting a ............... | | | | | |
| My Overall Rating | | | | | |

# Key 2

# Safety Self-Assessment Rating

**1: Needs More Work**     **2: Communicated**
**3: Buy-In**                    **4: Great Start**

| Stage 2 | 1 | 2 | 3 | 4 | Notes |
|---|---|---|---|---|---|
| **Safety is** exhibited through psychological, physical, social, and emotional practices. | | | | | |
| I understand how do manage conflict and the sources of conflict. | | | | | |
| Positive feedback utilizes Co-Active Coaching to develop an individual's emotional strength. | | | | | |
| Corrective feedback is used in a respectful and instructive manner so participants are encouraged and motivated to act. | | | | | |
| A socially responsible environment where participants are encouraged to take risks and learn from trial and error is formed due to modeling and feedback provided. | | | | | |

| | | | | |
|---|---|---|---|---|
| Leaders foster strong (psychological, physical, social, and emotional) team bonds for high-performance to occur by developing situational learning for teams to participate in. | | | | |
| Leaders create fun and motivating learning environments to reduce stress by having a clear perspective. | | | | |
| Leaders are perceived as caring, supportive, and motivational leaders concerned for the safety and well-being of the team and individuals. | | | | |
| The team members rated this meeting a ............... | | | | |
| My Overall Rating | | | | |

# Key 3

# Situational Learning Self-Assessment Rating

**1: Needs More Work**    **2: Communicated**
**3: Buy-In**             **4: Great Start**

| Stage 3 | 1 | 2 | 3 | 4 | Notes |
|---|---|---|---|---|---|
| A positive learning culture is formed as the leader uses games, trial and error, and experiential learning providing new opportunities for participants to engage and try. | | | | | |
| The leader communicates the evaluation process to motivate participants. | | | | | |
| Strength based approaches are used to foster growth and development. | | | | | |
| Knowledge is facilitated throughout the organization rather than seen as the experts of knowledge. | | | | | |
| Participants engage in the material and have time to process the information. | | | | | |
| Participants are building internal representation of the knowledge and interpretation of personal experience gained. Leaders engineer situations for individuals and teams to problem | | | | | |

| | | | | |
|---|---|---|---|---|
| solve by providing an atmosphere of trial and error through practice. Members learn to deal with conflict, engage in problem solving, and seek positive solutions. By nurturing leadership potential, through social-constructivist practices, high-performing teams are formed due to participants critically engaging in the subject. | | | | |
| Participants are assigned new problems, situations, and experiences to problem solve and learn. | | | | |
| Relationships are formed to foster motivation so feedback can be provided. | | | | |
| The leader communicates the evaluation process to motivate participants. | | | | |
| Participants are encouraged to have fun learning, and motivated to improve and share knowledge with their peers. | | | | |
| Mistakes are seen as opportunities for learning. | | | | |

# Key 4

# Partnerships Self-Assessment Rating

**1: Needs More Work**     **2: Communicated**
**3: Buy-In**     **4: Great Start**

| Stage 4 | 1 | 2 | 3 | 4 | Notes |
|---|---|---|---|---|---|
| Members share a common identity and work from a common set of beliefs. | | | | | |
| Members work together synchronously and asynchronously (as opposed to working in isolation) in order to accomplish tasks. | | | | | |
| The members believe the group is capable and will be successful. | | | | | |
| Authentic Learning Team members believe in the art of possibilities. | | | | | |
| Everyone understands who belongs as part of the group and who does not (i.e. membership). | | | | | |
| The roles or contributions of individual group members are openly recognized, celebrated, and appreciated. | | | | | |
| Tasks are balanced throughout the group with each member getting some "piece of the action." | | | | | |

| | | | | | |
|---|---|---|---|---|---|
| Feelings of trust exist within the and among group members. | | | | | |
| The group's work environment is joyful or positive; there is a sense of optimism and excitement. | | | | | |
| Conflict among group members is openly dealt with; it is not allowed to be ignored. | | | | | |
| All group members have access and openly share information; no one is left "out of the loop." | | | | | |
| During work sessions, group discourse is marked by high levels of active listening as well as question-asking. | | | | | |
| Stress is managed by the group so that it is not so high as to cause group paralysis and not so low that it doesn't induce productive group work. | | | | | |
| Risk-taking is encouraged while errors are tolerated and seen as opportunities for growth. | | | | | |
| Group members share a willingness to be flexible and a desire to be responsive to external input; Authentic Team Members are resilient to change | | | | | |

| | | | | | |
|---|---|---|---|---|---|
| Members understand and accept the group's organizational structure and operational format. | | | | | |
| Sessions" address individual concerns about process or behaviors. | | | | | |
| Reflection/journaling is a daily practice used to monitor progress. | | | | | |

The team members rated this meeting a _____

# Key 5

# Delegates Responsibility Self-Assessment Rating

**1: Needs More Work**   **2: Communicated**
**3: Buy-In**            **4: Great Start**

| Stage 4 | 1 | 2 | 3 | 4 | Notes |
|---|---|---|---|---|---|
| Clear guidelines are provided for participants to follow | | | | | |
| Communication is effective | | | | | |
| The use of leaders can be seen to lead project teams | | | | | |
| Leaders reflect on personal assumptions, transfer insight and knowledge, engage in the process of problem solving, and they collaboratively work to solve problems | | | | | |
| Participants learn to develop, practice, monitor, and attain goals | | | | | |
| Tools and resources are provided to develop future leaders, and to enhance leadership skills. The leader engages in mentoring others | | | | | |
| Leaders mentor and check progress of goals | | | | | |

| | | | | |
|---|---|---|---|---|
| Leader challenge old assumptions by modeling and questioning outdated practices | | | | |
| Action learning cycles are formed to check for progress and improvement | | | | |
| A learning culture is formed and promotes and delegates responsibilities to strengthen individuals, teams, and subsequently the organization | | | | |
| Teamwork and interdependence are seen as individuals work collaboratively to reach individual and team goals | | | | |
| The team members rated this meeting a ............... | | | | |
| My Overall Rating | | | | |

## Process Reflections

1. Why does your team exist?

2. What is our statement of belief toward which you can all work?

3. What do you do together?

4. What common tasks do you share?

5. Does your team create a positive environment that emphasizes success?

6. Does your team believe in a higher power/spiritual force? Can you describe what that looks like?

## Composition

7.  Who constitutes the group?

8.  Who attends and participates in the group? Does it bother you when members don't attend and don't participate? Describe how you feel.

9.  How does each team member know he/she is needed?

10. To what degree do team members exhibit behaviors that demonstrate trust? Can you describe those behaviors?

11. How do you recognize when a member is being vulnerable? Does this happen often?

12. What do you do when a member cannot be trusted?

13. Do you let hidden conflicts fester?

14. Do your norms support open conflict?

15. Does the team foster innovation and risk? In what ways does the group encourage risk-taking?

## Structure & Content

16. Do all team members understand and accept the team structure? How has this been communicated?

17. Do all team members feel fulfilled in the current team structure? How can you tell?

18. Does the team take "time outs" throughout the course of their meeting to debrief feelings and check understandings?

19. Does the team continually and carefully assess its environment?

# Notes: Designed Knowledge

<table>
<tr><td></td><td></td></tr>
</table>

# Notes: Designed Actions

# Notes: Designed Alliances

1)

2)

3)

Printed in the United States
by Baker & Taylor Publisher Services